SAILING WITH BOGIE

A Memoir of Humphrey Bogart's Passion for the Sea

By Larry Dudley

Second Edition   September 2010
ISBN: 9781453807484

Humphrey Bogart's SANTANA under way off Newport Harbor.

CONTENTS

Foreword

Author Larry Dudley has been called a "sailor's sailor," the kind of guy you want driving your boat when the wind is howling and visibility is zero: Mr. Calm and Collected.

Larry never raised his voice no matter how dicey the situation was. The tone of his deep baritone voice complimented his handsome, tanned and weathered features. Well over six feet, Larry instilled confidence in the rest of us mortals who sailed with him.

Larry's sailing career began when he was ten in 1930 when he bought his first sailboat. His mother bought the sails for him and he road his bike the 15 miles from Whittier, CA to Long Beach to sail her. As a teenager, Larry crewed on race boats, eventually hired as the skipper on the 56ft. yawl *TEVA* in the Sea of Cortez when he was just 18. In 1939 he crewed aboard the winning boat CONTENDER in the world famous Transpac race from Los Angeles to Hawaii.

When the Second World War broke out, Larry joined the Coast Guard and began a distinguished career under fire on the water surviving 23 major bombing attacks by the enemy. He ferried supplies ashore on LST's in Africa, Europe and the Pacific and at 23 became the youngest chief boatswain's mate in the Coast Guard. Larry saw action from Sicily to Saipan and even to Iwo Jima, he personally witnessed the famous Marine Corps flag raising on Mt. Suribachi.

After the war Larry continued his education and was working as a salesman when he got the fateful call from Hollywood's leading man; but Larry wasn't buying it. The voice on the phone said "Hello. This is Humphrey Bogart."

"Sure" Larry replied with a tone of sarcastic disbelief, "and this is Queen Victoria!" Thus began a ten year friendship that brought the two men as close as brothers.

Larry sailed with some of the finest sailors on the ocean, Irving Johnson, Commodore Tompkins, Dave Fraser, Gary Mull, Tom Schock, Baldwin A. Baldwin and Larry's long time friend Sterling Hayden. He did boat deliveries from Europe to North America and up and down the West Coast. Larry sailed in any number of world class races on world class boats. He raced with the late Roy Disney on PYEWACKET among others. In all, he traveled close to 400,000 miles on several oceans.

During the Bogart years Larry and his first wife Carol raised four wonderful children. Larry was thirty-six when Bogie died. He spent the next forty-five years close to sailing and the boats he loved. He was the quintessential sailor, knew something about every boat that had ever been built, they were like people to him. He gave up his position with International Rectifier and began to work in an area that he loved as National Sales Manager for Catalina Yachts. This eventually led to the opening of Larry Dudley Yacht Sales with his wife Ann in 1980 in Ventura Harbor, California.

He wrote *"Sailing With Bogie"* as a tribute to his dear friend with whom he had such a strong bond. That bond was best described in a conversation between the two aboard SANTANA sailing in a full moon and a fresh breeze.

"You know, Larry, I just can't seem to explain to people what it's like to be out here. It's beyond words...they'll never understand."

All Larry could think of was to quote softly, "*The way of a ship with the sea, the way of a man with a maid....* "

Larry Dudley passed away on August 24, 2001.

Larry Dudley and Humphrey Bogart aboard SANTANA.

THE PHONE CALL FROM NEWPORT HARBOR

The phone rang in Federated Metals' grubby warehouse office. I stuffed a bite of lunch in my mouth and mumbled "Shipping".

"Is this Larry Dudley?" A distinctive, slightly raspy voice, doing a nice Bogart imitation. "This is Humphrey Bogart."

"And I'm Queen Victoria," I retorted.

Bogie later told me he almost hung up at that point.

"Bob Brokaw gave me your number, said you might want to crew on SANTANA in a race next week." <u>Migod that's true!</u> I remembered I had told Bob I was looking for a good boat to sail on occasionally. He had said he might know someone who could use me, but hadn't said who.

I had admired SANTANA since she was launched at Wilmington Boat Works in 1935, had even sailed a couple of times with her first owner when she was still a schooner. Re-rigged as a yawl during WWII, she had belonged to Bogart since 1945. Now, in the late summer of 1947, he was asking me to sail again on one of the finest yachts I had ever known, with an already legendary captain.

"Of course I will - just tell me where and when!"

A few days later I drove to the Newport Harbor Yacht Club and joined Bogart's crew - for nearly ten years.

My first sail with Bogie on SANTANA was a short local race - not much wind, a crew that was competent but not cohesive. Still, it was enjoyable and I thought I had done well enough to be asked again, but several months went by before we ran into each other at the Bay Club in Newport and he said, "I've been meaning to call you - can you go with us in the San Clemente Island race next week?"

I had seen Humphrey Bogart and nodded "Hello" to him on my infrequent visits to the Newport Harbor Yacht Club, where he seemed to be comfortable. He knew many of the members and had a reputation for good work on protest

2

committees handling complaints about fouls during races. He had studied the rules and raced a little Dyer dinghy and then a 21 foot Albatross sloop to the bay championship in 1944, beating a former champion. Most of the protests to sound each other out and find that in our own fields, in our own ways, each of us had paid his dues and we could trust each other. He was a *proud* man, but not too proud to learn from anyone who could teach him. He just could not stand stuffed shirts or people who took money for acting but protested that they really weren't actors. He was proud to be an actor and he wanted to sail with men who were proud to be sailors.

Although he had sailed a little on Lake Canandaigua during summers in New York when he was small, Bogie was virtually a beginner in sail when he re-entered boating during the Second World War by joining the Newport Harbor Yacht Club, and the conflicts between his ego, basic cynicism, irreverent dislike of stuffed shirts and the "old boy" network operating in many clubs made for some touchy situations.

3

It wasn't easy to be accepted at Newport or Los Angeles Yacht Clubs if you were an actor. Bogie went into Newport almost "cold," half hoping to be treated like any other new member. The first time he sat up to the bar the stuffy - looking older man on the next stool only made light conversation. Apparently he didn't recognize Bogie, and their talk died.

A bit annoyed, Bogie finally said, "My name's Bogart."
"I'm Ralph - own a Newporter ketch."

Long pause. Bogart pushed on.
"I'm an actor." No reaction ... "I was in *Casablanca.* "
Ralph was polite. "That's very interesting. Never been out of the States myself."
Bogie roared with laughter, jumped off his stool, threw his arms around Ralph and ordered drinks. He never was sure whether he had been put on by a master, or if Ralph really didn't know who he was, but it didn't matter. They became good

4

friends.

Several years later a self-important commodore, headed for a Board meeting, found the whole SANTANA crew (including the paid hand, Carl Petersen) drinking together in the bar.

P. F. - the commodore - called Bogie aside to tell him that club policy did not allow "servants" to socialize in the clubhouse with members. Bogie tried to keep his temper as he pointed out that "Pete" was decently dressed, well behaved, "better than some of your members" - and his guest. P.F. was adamant - the paid hand had to go.

Finally Bogie grabbed a bar napkin and scribbled a note on the back. "Here's my resignation from the club" he said, folding it up and handing it to the commodore, who angrily shoved it in his pocket unread. A few minutes later P.F. opened the regular meeting of the Board of Directors by announcing that he was altering the usual order of business to

SANTANA crew pose at the Newport Harbor Yacht Club.

(Larry Dudley, Bob Marlott, John Freiburg, Humphrey Bogart, Dean Harrell, Kenny Watts, George Roosevelt, Jr. –Seated from left Carl Petersen and Robert Dorris

take up a serious matter that had just come to his attention. He pulled out the crumpled napkin and began to read aloud.

"I, Humphrey Bogart, hereby resign from this yacht club because the commodore is a stupid, pompous sonuvabitch who .... " P.F.'s voice choked and trailed off.

"We can take this up at a later time," he stammered.

It was never brought up again.

Dick Edwards, known as "Whispering Dick" because his conversational level was close to a shout, was involved in a NHYC episode that Bogie treasured. He and Bogie were alike in their enjoyment of drinking, their sense of fun and their deep dislike of P.F.

At the club's annual awards dinner they found a way to get at him by using the oldest, most respected, ready-to-retire waiter. The frail looking, white haired man, a sizeable tip in his pocket, overloaded a huge tray with dirty dishes, half-full cups of coffee, glasses and trash, and waited, out of sight, for a signal from Bogie and Dick.

As P.F. droned on and on with his dull keynote speech the members began to realize that the waiter- very slowly crossing in front of the head table with his heaping tray- was swaying and dangerously close to dumping it on the floor, or on the speakers' table. No one paid any attention to the commodore. All eyes were glued on the waiter, who staggered and recovered several times before he reached the scullery door and received a hearty round of applause. P.F.'s evening was ruined. He could never prove there had been a conspiracy, but he knew in his heart Bogart and Edwards had done it.

Bogie bought a small power cruiser named SLUGGY, which was the scene of legendary battles. He and his third wife, Mayo Methot, were both seriously devoted to drinking and fighting. Perhaps it was to get away from the narrow confines of SLUGGY, harbor-bound by the war, that he began sailing dinghies in Newport Harbor.

Humphrey Bogart, as sailor as well as actor, was a "quick study". In a year he graduated into the 21 foot Albatross sloop class, which had attracted many of the bay's best sailors. With a minimum of coaching, and hard study of the rules, he learned so well that he was asked to serve on protest committees at Newport Harbor Yacht Club and he won the class championship in 1944, beating a former Star class world champion. When the bay opened at the end of the war Bogie had gotten rid of Mayo. Both of them were tired of fighting and Bogie had fallen deeply in love with Lauren Bacall, his co-star in *To Have and Have Not*. He once told me, "All Mayo really wanted was enough money to go back to Oregon and drink herself to death - and I gave it to her." He wasn't proud of doing it, but it was a simple fact of life.

SANTANA sailing near Diamond Head in Hawaii.

SANTANA

SLUGGY and the little bay sloop were sold and after buying his dream ship, SANTANA, from Dick Powell on December 3, 1945, he and his young wife spent most weekends aboard her.

Sailing means something different to everyone who does it, from a casual flirtation with the wind to a deeply important, essential part of life. Bogart already had a full life when he bought SANTANA - success in his profession, a beautiful young wife whom he adored, a family to start and raise, but there was something unique that sailing SANTANA gave him. It was the chance to be and do something real - not a role as a jet pilot, private eye, gangster, or whatever, but to really be in charge of a small ship and her crew, and acquit himself well. He had been competitive in golf and tennis, at club level, but he found a better challenge on the water.

SANTANA gave him a place where he could be a sailor

among sailors, master of a finite but complete world where he was at ease, accepted as a skilled helmsman, boat handler and sometime competitor.

Bogie could and did move freely in the sailing world. He was very rarely treated as a celebrity. He was a sailor - the word was out that he managed his boat and her crew well.

"Don't try any tricks on him - he knows the rules and he knows how to sail his boat!" Bogart's instinctive grasp of command made his crew feel confidence in him and each other. He soon developed a sense of style, of doing things as well as he could and doing them better as time went by. Sometimes he showed off a little, but not foolishly - he just stretched his skill by taking minor chances that raised our pulses a bit, rather than doing it the easy way each time. He liked challenges.

The Bogarts soon learned SANTANA could be a handful. A boat her size and rig can be sailed by a couple in settled weather in familiar waters, but it takes more than two or three people to manage her when it blows hard or anchor or reefing lines have to be hauled. Racing, when several minor crises can happen simultaneously, called for even more experienced crew. Bogie and Betty (what Bogie called Lauren) did sail from Newport to Catalina, where they had bought a mooring in Moonstone Cove, without additional hands, but he knew it wasn't a wise thing to do.

When he first bought SANTANA Bogie took advice and coaching from Peggy Slater, a well known sailor and an old friend of mine. He enlisted respected men like the famous sailmaker Kenny Watts and naval architect Bill Lapworth to crew in occasional races, and gradually assembled a list of shipmates - sailors who were sometimes available, and could get along in close quarters. SANTANA was sailed better and better as Bogie and his crew learned her ways for several years, and learned to know and trust each other.

13

In sailing "size makes speed." Over a period of time a good big boat will beat a good little boat, so measurement rules and time allowances had to be developed that attempt to equalize this inherent disparity and allow mixed sizes and types to race together, especially in offshore events. SANTANA was built to conform to the CCA (Cruising Club of America) rule that had been in effect in the United States since the late 1920's, based on measurements of many yachts generally considered to be desirable combinations of speed, livability, seakindliness, good looks and sound, conservative engineering.

No creation is perfect - clever designers can find loopholes in any rule, but for years the CCA fostered the building of yachts that have become classics. SANTANA was one of them, almost from her launching in 1935 - a remarkable vessel that combined the best talents of designer Olin Stephens, Jr. (only in his mid twenties when he drew her lines) and Hugh Angleman, who ran the finest boatyard in California. She was less than ten years old when Bogart bought her, but already

14

considered a classic for her good looks, superb construction and racing record. Completely aside from the glamour of her movie star owners, she is one of the great yachts; no fine boat can be counted an inanimate thing, but she has a better soul than most - a model of temperance, strength, dignity and romance that gave her crew a sense of camaraderie we treasured.

SANTANA had been admired and respected nationally ever since she was built for William L. Stewart, Jr., then president of Union Oil Company, and she had proved to be as good a schooner as any in competition. Bill Stewart sailed her to second in fleet in the 1936 Transpac Race to Hawaii and won the schooner class in the 1937 race from Newport, Rhode Island to Bermuda. (Stewart had shipped her east on the deck of one of his tankers). But SANTANA was sold several times in the next few years, as WWII began and sailing outside harbors was forbidden. Little yacht work was done in the boatyards, but while George Brent owned her Angleman squeezed in a rework of SANTANA to a yawl rig and removed her bowsprit. It wasn't possible to get the spruce for the taller main mast specified by Olin Stephens, so

the original schooner mast was moved forward. For cruising and

racing in ordinary conditions the resulting sail area was

adequate, but she was never a good light air

performer. Bogie considered a new or extended mast,

corresponded with Stephens about the 8' taller one strongly

recommended by the country's leading yacht designer, but never

did it.

He was reluctant to give up the ease of handling

SANTANA's moderate rig, and her splendid power when it blew

hard, for a better chance in light airs. "Sailing with the equivalent

of one deep reef all the time, we still win some, and she doesn't

need much sail changing or reefing when we're cruising," Bogie

told me after getting one of Olin's annual pleas for the taller

mast.

In the first years Betty Becall made a valiant effort to

share her husband's love of sailing. She even went along as cook

for a crew of hungry sailors in a slow 120 mile race to Ensenada

16

in Mexico. They remember the look of utter disgust on her face on the third morning when she came up from the cramped, almost airless galley and asked "How do you fellas want your goddam eggs?" But much as she loved her husband, it gradually became clear Betty was finding more and more reasons to not make the long pre-freeway drive to Newport Harbor in Orange County. She had a child and a home to manage, a career in high gear, and lots of friends in the motion picture world whom she found much more entertaining than the motley crew of SANTANA.

We gradually realized she was not going to be aboard very much, but Bogie never completely lost hope of sharing this side of his life with her. Even later, when it seemed Memorial Day, the Fourth of July and Labor Day were the only times she was likely to come along, he still did everything he could to make it fun for her.

The paid sailor who maintained SANTANA - Ted

Howard for several years, then Carl Petersen - and the cook,

usually Roger, got a series of calls to impress on them the need

to have the ship and menu in perfect order. (Bogie had given up

on Betty's cooking, which relied heavily on Beef Stroganoff).

Knowing it was in many ways the toughest job onboard,

he finally hired a cook for most weekends and all overnight

racing.

The Bogarts worked out an informal, practical

compromise. He told us that Betty expected him to leave home

for the boat on Friday after cocktails, and to return Sunday

evening. He was available for parenting, socializing or whatever

she wanted until the next Friday. "She gets five nights,

SANTANA gets two," he said. "Seems fair, doesn't it?"

As Betty's strong presence began to fade from

SANTANA the situation on board changed. The portside bunk in

the aft cabin was no longer held sacred. Regular crew members

began to sleep in it, across a five foot space from Bogie, and

those who passed his tests were welcome.

First, you had to be able to sleep near a compulsive reader, who could devour a book a night, and sometimes wanted to talk about it.

Second, you could not be a loud snorer, though Bogie himself was not entirely blameless in this regard.

Third, you had to be deeply devoted to SANTANA and her people.

Humphrey Bogart and Lauren "Betty" Becall in Portofino, Italy.

"Portofino's best. Sorry – not like Newport. Capt. Quieg"

THE AFRICAN QUEEN

The reading part, and talking about almost anything, was easy for me. I snored much less than the other regular, Bob Marlatt, and my love of the ship was as great as our captain's, so I began to spend more time in Betty's bunk.

One Saturday night SANTANA was moored in her usual place in Moonstone Cove at Catalina. I was reading a paperback novel and Bogie was deeply into Vanderbilt's classic text on yacht racing. He was a fast and efficient reader, seeming to quickly extract the meat from any book. There were several points in Vanderbilt that he wanted to talk about for a few minutes, before we lapsed back into our separate books.

By midnight I had nearly finished mine, and jokingly said to Bogie, "There's a good part in this for you, if you were a better actor and could play a Cockney." He peered over his Ben Franklin reading glasses and grunted, "Toss it over when you're through." A few moments later I did, then rolled over on my side

21

to sleep.

About one thirty, I awoke to find Bogie still reading. He looked over at me with a mischievous glint in his eyes and asked, "He could be a Canadian, couldn't he?"

By three he had finished "*The African Queen*," and before eight a marine radio operator in San Pedro was putting a phone link through to John Huston's castle in Ireland. Bogie said, "Remember, John, you owe me a picture." This was apparently a standing arrangement; whenever either one had a project that needed the other he claimed he was "owed" one.

"Before you tell me about yours, Bogie, I've GOT to tell you about mine - I was going to call you when you got off that damn boat. There's a C. S. Forester book called "*The African Queen*" that's perfect for you and Hepburn. Sam Spiegel has the rights.... " Bogie started laughing, "That's the same book I just read! Do you think we can get Kate?" And they agreed to try to make the picture as soon as they could work out schedules.

Our captain's career was seldom talked about aboard SANTANA, unless a shooting schedule interfered with a race, or vice versa. I was not surprised that the next I heard about the African picture was in December 1949, a few weeks before he and Betty left for the Congo location.

Carol and I had been asked, very casually, to drop by the Benedict Canyon home Christmas morning. About 11 o'clock we drove up to a very silent house. No other cars were parked outside and Fred, the usually unflappable butler, seemed surprised at our arrival. He disappeared to announce us.

We waited alone in the living room, which obviously had been the scene of a large and raucous party. Gag presents, most of them connected in some way to the African trip, were strewn around, and unfinished drinks stood on tables. In a few minutes Bogie came in, wearing a bathrobe, a genuine pith helmet and a bedraggled look. He had a classic hangover, and we were sure he had completely forgotten his invitation, but his basic good manners took over. We spent a slightly awkward half hour, Bloody Marys in hand, talking to him and Betty, who was completely mystified by our presence. Bogie did say that the previous night's event was sort of a going away party combined with his birthday, and the house was too small for them to invite everyone they wanted. Somehow Bogie made us feel that being there with just the two of them was much better, and he wanted us to know how glad they were that we had remembered to come by! Betty, who almost never lost her composure, was having a hard time keeping a straight face as we went out the door.

The making of *The African Queen* has been described at length by Hepburn and Bacall in their books. There is little to add except some of Bogie's comments to SANTANA's crew after it was completed. He was proud of the picture and his part in it, but he always felt that if he deserved an Academy award, it should have been for *Treasure of the Sierra Madre*. He was also proud of the fact that when the expert boat handler who was expected to manage the complex logistics of the QUEEN's river runs came down with severe dysentery and went home to

24

England, he had filled in and helped Huston with some difficult shots.

He loved telling about the night they left natives to watch the AFRICAN QUEEN, with strict instructions to never take their eyes off it. When the film crew found it in the morning, sunk at its mooring next to the bank, the watchmen insisted they had faithfully watched it sink, and they were genuinely puzzled to be blamed for anything.

Bogie had gotten very tired of surviving in Africa on peanut butter and Scotch. He hated the leeches, even the rubber ones finally used, and the cold water in the tank in England.

He loved and admired Katherine Hepburn, saying "If it wasn't for Betty and Spence I'd try to get her to fall in love with me." He talked about having me meet Kate, since both of us seemed to know at least a little about all sorts of things. "You'd probably argue like hell," he muttered, eyes gleaming at idea of promoting conflict. Pitting people, even his friends, against each other was always fun for him. The Bogarts asked Carol and me

25

to attend the premiere screening at the Academy's theater on Melrose. Perhaps it was a gesture based on our mutual first reading of the book - for whatever reason, we all went together in Betty's car.

As a backer of the film Bogie was still mad at Sam Spiegel about some of the costs assessed against it, especially a huge fee ("extortion," he called it) for bringing the print from London to Hollywood in time for this showing, but he quickly forgot that as the lights went down and the picture began. He had not seen the complete, final cut. Sitting next to Bogie I could feel his excitement and pride as everyone in the theater began to sense this was a real winner. The print was perfect, and nearly fifteen minutes longer than usually shown today. More time was given to the scenes with Robert Morley in the mission, there was more river action footage, and the love scenes between Bogie and Kate were fuller. By the final few feet of film there was a palpable feeling that we had just seen a classic, and the applause was loud and long at the end. We were very proud of our friend, and we rode the few blocks to the party at Romanoff's in a euphoric haze.

Everyone who works on a film is a contributor; there is no creative effort more of a collaboration, but it all starts with ideas and words in someone's head. Knowing Bogie's respect for writers and his many friendships with them it wasn't surprising to meet the novelist C.S Forester, and James Agee, who wrote the screenplay. Somehow those writers were more important to me than any of the stars and producers and directors there. Forester said he started wondering what his maiden aunt would have done in a setting completely different from her mundane real life and the story just grew, almost by itself. Agee said little about his work in shaping and polishing the novel into a great screenplay. In spite of his reputation he seemed ill at ease, not a natural part of the movie scene. Carol and I were also outsiders, but we thoroughly enjoyed the evening, so different from our suburban life in Whittier! At least we hadn't embarrassed our hosts.....

Humphrey Bogart joking around on the deck.

THE MOVE TO LAYC

When the Bogarts returned from Africa they were very tired, and he had lost at least ten pounds he never regained. The crew had kept SANTANA sailing in a few races, but it wasn't the same without him and we were glad to have our real captain back. We could get her to move pretty well; we won an occasional race without Bogie, but it wasn't as much fun. He sailed her better.

Betty kept pressure on her husband to move from Benedict Canyon, which she considered a wilderness. The house was too small for the growing family, had little parking space, and she was sure the nearby chaparral harbored rattlesnakes, coyotes and other wild creatures to threaten children. She started looking for a better house in a more civilized location.

Bogie wanted SANTANA closer to his home, raising the chances of getting his wife aboard and cutting down on the increasingly long and dreary drive to Newport Harbor. He began to consider joining Los Angeles Yacht club, which had no slips, no bar or dining room, only a simple Spartan clubhouse on a mole jutting into Los Angeles harbor from Terminal Island in San Pedro Bay, less than half as far as Newport. It did have a national reputation as a sailor's club, with a lot of Pasadena influence and Union Oil executives and Transpac sailors among its members.

He had friends in LAYC, such as Ken Carey and Howard Wright, and the club was dominated by Bill Stewart and his CHUBASCO, the larger, newer version of SANTANA. With good words from friends and his Pasadena - based business manager, Morgan Maree, Bogie was accepted into LAYC, although there were the usual misgivings about an actor, and SANTANA found a berth at California Yacht Anchorage, near Fort MacArthur in San Pedro.

Before Leslie was born in August, 1952, they had settled

into a large, gracious home on Mapleton Drive in Holmby Hills.

Fred, the fawning butler, was gone, but the core of the staff was

there; May Smith, who had cooked for Bogie for many years,

and Mrs. Sloan, his secretary, who made many of the

arrangements with the crew. We had learned that she was a

legacy from an old New York friend. Bogie had created a job for

her years before and she was with him to stay, in spite of Betty's

exasperation with her genteel Southern manner, occasional

inefficiency, and insistence on being considered somewhat above

the cook and gardener.

May and Kathy Sloan were with Bogie for nearly twenty

years. Once you became a part of his life you _stayed_ in it unless

something caused him to lose faith in you. Ted Howard, a

talented professional seaman, could have spent the rest of his life

on SANTANA, but personal mental problems intervened,

although Bogie paid for much psychiatric counseling. After Ted

tried to commit suicide with a shotgun he had drunkenly loaded with .22 bullets, Bogie gave up and after a brief trial of another man, hired Carl "Pete" Petersen, who was a lesser sailor but could get along with nearly everyone, and Bogie kept him aboard in spite of Betty's complaints.

On the other hand, when he felt one of SANTANA'S early Newport crew had ripped him off over a dinghy, Bogie never spoke to, or about, him again, although the man's wife tried to become close to Betty. Real friends and loyal employees were with him for good, and he proved it many times. He had kept the same hairdresser tending "the rug," as he called his toupee, for many years. Perhaps Vera "Pete" Petersen (no relation to SANTANA's boatkeeper) had been his mistress during the Mayo years; she was still close to him, and visited aboard the yacht, but she never seemed a threat to the Bogart marriage. He was deeply in love with his wife, and she adored him.

Sterling Hayden, Betty Hayden and Humphrey Bogart on
SANTANA.

There was a distinct split in Bogie's life between the film star, husband of Lauren Bacall, and his other life as a sailor, the captain of SANTANA. Not many people bridged that gap - few of his buddies from Hollywood had any feeling for the sea and most of his crew was equally out of touch with films and acting.

He felt the dichotomy very deeply. One night we were crossing the rough channel between San Clemente and Catalina islands, sailing almost as fast as SANTANA could on a broad reach across the moon's path. Bogie was braced at the weather rail, watching and feeling his ship almost delicately shouldering her 22 tons through the waves, pressed on by 1300 square feet of taut Dacron sails.

He was silent for a long time, then with a sigh he quietly said to me, "They'll never understand - I've tried and tried to tell them, but they don't feel it...." All I could think of was to quote softly, "*The way of a ship with the sea, the way of a man with a maid....* "

So only a handful of film people sailed on Bogie's ship.

34

We would take one or two or three at a time out for harbor

excursions .... day sails, or "circumnavigation" of Terminal

island that involved opening a couple of bridges and a meeting

with a ferry. There were a few who either sailed well or were

such good company they were welcome unless we were racing.

Many of his friends were aboard for those afternoon

sails, or a single overnight at Catalina, but weren't invited again.

Not because he disliked them, but because they didn't fit in.

Mike Romanoff showed up wearing authentic-looking 1915 style

yachting clothes and carrying a large wicker basket full of

delicacies from his restaurant. We had fun and good food - but

he never came again.

Only a few actors sailed with us - Richard Greene or Jeff

Richards (sometimes); James Dean (once); Tony Curtis and

Janet Leigh on a cool winter afternoon. David Niven had a

special status. He was not really a sailor, but there was never a

finer shipmate. Keenan Wynn kept us laughing all the way to

Ensenada but he was bored by sailing and never returned.

Richard and Sybil Burton were aboard several times - Bogie found them entertaining, but he seemed to find most actors boring, at least aboard his boat. He usually preferred the company of writers and directors and people who had lives outside "the business," like the legendary pilot Charlie Blair, who had pioneered the airlines' use of the jet stream, or Charles Grayson of ESQUIRE who was great at word games.

The crew - those who were more or less regularly aboard - meant the paid hands (Ted Howard or Carl Petersen, and the cook, usually Roger) and one or two from a list that included Ken Carey, Bob Dorris, George Roosevelt, Dean Harrell, John Freiberg, Bob Marlatt and myself. We were lawyer, boat designer, stockbroker, paint manufacturer, advertising executives and metal salesman, all sailors who would spot a sail on the horizon and happily argue for fifteen minutes about what boat it was.

He sometimes called SANTANA "the other side of my life," and part of him wanted to keep it separate, but Bogie could not help bringing aboard bits from his work in films. He might not say a word to his crew for weeks or months about the picture he was shooting, then tell a series of stories about his co-star or the director, or about the producer of a film he made years before. We even heard tales about his nearly twenty years as jack-of-many parts in the theater and 12 movies, as stage manager of road companies, understudying most of the male roles, and as an aging juvenile. He had learned to memorize lines, listen to directors, keep cool when someone blew up in a scene.

"For Larry, Marlott and Santana crew...
Your beloved bastard Skipper"

One of his favorite memories was of the time Alice Brady, the leading lady of a traveling production, left him alone on stage. The star, known for her eccentricities and weak bladder, walked off in the middle of their scene without warning or explanation. He heard her steps clanging on the iron spiral staircase that led up to her dressing room, then the door shut.

"I stood there, VERY alone, in a living room set, with no lines to say. It was the loneliest, most frightening moment you can imagine. Then inspiration hit me. There were shelves full of books all around the room, and I croaked, 'You can tell a lot about people by the books they have.' I slowly began to read titles and I was halfway through one shelf when I heard the faint sound of a flushing toilet, and Miss Brady's steps coming down the iron spiral.

"She walked on, picked up her next line as if she had never left, and we finished the scene," he said, very proud of not panicking on stage no matter what went wrong.

The theater people he had met during his apprenticeship - Robert Sherwood, Leland Hayward, Clifton Webb, Spencer Tracy, and especially Leslie Howard - were always important to him. Learning his trade, developing the discipline and skills to do the job well, earning the respect of his associates - these were basic to Bogie's approach to acting, and to sailing.

He once told us about Leslie Howard's concentration on even the simplest things. After they worked together on Broadway in *The Petrified Forest* Howard had resurrected Bogie's movie career by telling Warner he would not make the picture unless Bogie played Duke Mantee. As in the play, the picture's main action takes place on a single set, a desert roadside cafe/bar, and the set designer almost duplicated the Broadway one. Bogie felt at home on it, but he returned early from a lunch break to find Howard practicing his first entrance and cross to center stage.

"Leslie had played that scene a hundred times. Why was he taking his own time to walk across, over and over and over?

40

He must have done it fifty times! Finally I asked him what he

was doing, and he quietly told me he had realized this set was

slightly wider and deeper than the stage one, so he would have to

re-think and re-time his entrance and cross. Bogie said, "He was

making sure his move looked unstudied and natural - and when

we shot it, that's what it had become!"

The Bogarts' only daughter is named Leslie.

Like many of the actors who were locked into the studio

system, forced by iron-clad contracts to make whatever films

they were assigned by Louis Mayer or Harry Cohn or Jack

Warner or other studio heads, Bogie enjoyed opportunities to get

back at them - and still keep working.

Warner was his favorite target. As head of Warner

Brothers he had been Bogie's boss for years and they had tangled

over casting and billing and selection of stories many times.

Once Bogart came into Preston Sturges' restaurant on Sunset

Boulevard, bleeding from a cut hand he had wrapped in a towel, and announced that he had just killed Jack Warner. There was applause before people realized Bogie was drunk and had cut his hand on a broken highball glass, but a lot of them were with him in spirit.

Jack seemed to have a gift for antagonizing creative people, boasting that he often didn't even read the outline of a proposed picture and relied on descriptions from a would-be producer or the director or a writer, and his own instincts.

John Huston had made money for Warners before WW II with *The Maltese Falcon*, so Jack listened to the director as he described a sort of Mexican-Western called *Treasure of the Sierra Madre*. The story he made up and outlined had little to do with the book by B. Traven that Huston intended to film, but Warner felt safe enough with it, saying "Westerns always make money." He intended to keep an eye on the production, insisting that daily rushes be sent to him from the remote location.

A few days after shooting started he received a long, repetitious, series of shots of the rear end of a pack burro going up a steep, rocky, dusty trail somewhere in the Sierra Madre. For days John and Bogie kept sending more of the same footage, and nothing else. Finally Warner sent a frantic telegram demanding that Huston get the damn mule to the top before the studio went broke!

Huston and Bogart disagreed about the so-called "translator," an uninvited character who drifted in and out of the location. John thought he wasn't the mysterious B. Traven; Bogie was sure he was. "There was no doubt about it!" he told me firmly, eyes sparkling at the memory of arguing with John.

Being with John and Walter Huston on location for *Treasure* was one of his favorite times in making movies. He admired both of them, and loved having Betty there, but John's slow pace finally took the picture past the deadline for sailing the 1947 race to Hawaii.

Bogie had been promised it would be finished in time. He never trusted John's schedules again, and was not really surprised later when *The African Queen* had serious problems with Huston's mood swings and wandering attention.

To sail SANTANA more than two thousand miles to Honolulu had been part of Bogie's dream ever since he bought her. Not doing it then was a deep disappointment, but there was a race every two years and he never again really tried to enter. We talked about it once and he said, "It comes at a time - early July - when I'm almost always working, a lot of good actors are more available in summer, and usually outdoor shooting is best done in May, June, July .... Besides, I'm not as sure now as I was in 1947 that I'd want to be at sea with you guys for two solid weeks!" The subject was never brought up again. He seemed to have realized that dream was best left alone....

Drinking was a well-established part of Bogie's life from his early twenties. Long before we met sailing on SANTANA he had somehow learned to steer a careful course between his fondness for liquor and his life of acting on stage and in films. When he fell in love with Betty it was at the end of a disastrous marriage full of booze, during which he had made several of his most memorable pictures, such as *The Maltese Falcon* and *Casablanca*, without a problem that seriously interfered with his work. The drinking eased up when they married and had children, but he felt that off the set, relaxing with his wife and his friends, he could sometimes try to catch up with "A world one drink behind."

Larry Dudley (2nd from left sitting) and Humphrey Bogart (last on right sitting) and crew sailing in light winds.

Aboard SANTANA we never saw him drink before or during a race, or underway, except a token highball at five with the whole crew. Nobody got another drink until the ship was moored safely - then we had several. Bogie usually drank a weak Scotch and a drink lasted him a long time. There were people who believed he was a terrible lush because they thought he always had a drink in his hand. They didn't know how he had nursed that drink, sometimes for hours.

Usually he knew his limits. Once he and I sat at a bar before a crew meeting, one of the few planned ones we ever had. I ordered a very dry Martini - a drink we seldom saw aboard SANTANA - and Bogie said wistfully, "I'd love to have one too, but I don't dare. Used to drink them, and I always got in trouble." Of course, I thought, you can pace yourself on a Scotch and soda, but it's hard to sip a good Martini for an hour or two ....

There were times when Captain Bogart overdid it. We were rowing back to SANTANA in the tipsy Lehman dinghy he liked so well because it was a fine sailor, very late one dark night

47

in Moonstone Cove, returning from too long an evening aboard Paul Mantz's big motorsailer PEZ ESPADA.

Bogie suddenly stood up, shouted "There's the ship," and tried to walk across 20 feet of water. Since he was wearing his favorite heavy sailing coat he began to sink like a rock. It took a lot of effort by two of us to get him to the boarding ladder and up on deck, and we were all sobered by the close call.

There were lots of fun and games aboard SANTANA that did not involve drinking or pranks - word games like Scrabble, cards (Canasta and gin rummy), chess when a worthy opponent for Bogie was aboard. He was a better than average player who hated to lose at any game, so he was rather careful to pick adversaries who were good - but not too good.

Once I made the mistake of asking an old shipmate of mine, John Nicholas, to join the crew for a Channel Islands race. Not only did he have a different sailing philosophy than Bogie - John believed in easing off a little from the close-to-the-wind angle most of us favored, and going for more speed even though

48

it meant sailing farther - but when they sat down for a game of Canasta he said had never played it but would like to learn.

Bogie shot a quizzical look at me, since I had told him John was a very good card player, based on my memory of his cleaning up aboard CONTENDER and SALLY years before. A little miffed, Bogie explained the game to this "beginner," not understanding that John was a real genius at any card game, even one at which he had no experience. He remembered every card that showed, and absorbed the rules and strategies of Canasta immediately, so in a couple of hours he had won everything.

"This is a fun game! I'm glad you showed it to me ... " he beamed happily. Bogie glared at me, and a few minutes later when we were alone said, "Don't ever bring him again!"

Of course Scrabble, before the days of special dictionaries, meant loud, heated arguments about the admissibility of weird words and weirder spellings. Bogie was a good bluffer who tried to get away with a lot, but we fought hard to keep him honest.

Living accommodations for guests on SANTANA were surprisingly Spartan and scanty. The owner's cabin aft had two good single berths separated by an engine cover that masqueraded as a dresser, but the main cabin slept only four, in two raised single pilot berths and two single settees, and there was only one toilet room - the "head"- shared by everyone except the paid crew, who had two narrow pipe berths and their own toilet in the bow forward of the galley.

Sometimes people found it hard to sleep a few feet from two or three total strangers, and their privacy was violated every time someone from the master's cabin wanted a snack or a drink in the middle of the night, which meant a walk through the salon where four people might be sleeping.

This sort of intimacy is common, almost expected, on sailing yachts of SANTANA's era and size. The regulars thought nothing of it and managed to maintain a certain poise about the inevitable odd meetings.

One night I was sleeping in the starboard pilot berth,

50

across from Carol in the port one. Just after dawn I realized Bogie had just passed through to the galley. He was being very quiet and considerate, probably thinking no one was awake yet, but Carol opened her eyes just as he came back, headed for his own cabin. Their eyes met. Bogie said, with as much aplomb as a naked actor could muster under the circumstances, "Good morning, Carol." She kept her eyes locked on his and replied, just as calmly, "Good morning, Bogie."

Neither of them ever mentioned the encounter later.

SANATANA at anchor at Santa Cruz Island.

THE ISLANDS

We sailed past Santa Cruz island, 20 miles offshore from Santa Barbara, several times in races, and finally anchored briefly in a small cove after we dropped out of an excruciatingly slow Channel Islands race. Bogie liked the course from Los Angeles around all the islands off the Southern California coast and return. A difficult, frequently frustrating affair because of night calms interspersed with heavy winds and rough seas near San Miguel island and Richardson Rock, it never attracted large fleets. But some of the best ocean racers of the time did enter, and Bogie felt it was SANTANA's kind of race.

This time the winds were so light we spent a whole night drifting off Santa Barbara after taking two days to beat up from Los Angeles. The whole crew was fed up. Comparisons were made between our progress and that of Juan Cabrillo 300 years before, when he was sailing a terrible, leaky caravel along the same coast.

It was a relief to all of us when we agreed to drop out of the race and get back home, but some also wanted to make a short stop at Santa Cruz. Bob Marlatt had spent many months around the island on a Coast Guard patrol vessel during the war and I had sailed the waters around it for several years. We combined to almost insist that SANTANA spend at least one night anchored in a cove there.

It was love at first sight for Bogie. High mountains, almost deserted anchorages with no mooring buoys, a wild coastline without a sign of man for miles made a vivid contrast with the softer, tamer channel side of Catalina and the popular coves where SANTANA usually went. We found a good spot in Little Scorpion cove, near the east end of the island, and settled in for a peaceful night, the pressures of racing behind us.

The next morning while it was still dark we began to hear a faint, plaintive bleating from somewhere on the island near us, and as dawn broke we could see, on a small ledge under a rugged cliff, a lamb that had fallen and was trapped,

54

surrounded by water and unable to climb back up. Its mother was the ewe we were hearing, standing where she could see her lamb, but helpless.

Bogie and I looked at each other and agreed we should launch the dinghy and row the hundred yards to the ledge. When I clambered onto it the lamb was bleeding from cuts made by the sharp rocks and shaking with exhaustion and fear. There was no resistance when I picked it up and handed it to Bogie, sitting in the stem of the little skiff with a three-day stubble of beard, grubby old clothes and bare feet.

He cradled the lamb in his arms, ignoring the blood and dirt, and held it close as I rowed a few yards to the little beach where the ewe was waiting for us, still bleating. When he put the lamb ashore it staggered up to its mother and they slowly moved inland, out of our sight.

It didn't seem wrong or stupid when Bogie said, "Makes you feel a little like Jesus Christ, doesn't it.... "

We wanted to come back, and Bogie asked me to see

about a landing permit, since most of Santa Cruz was privately

owned by Edwin Stanton, a crusty rancher without much love for

visitors. A few weeks later I called the Island Company's office

in Los Angeles and was surprised when Mr. Stanton himself

answered. When I told him the call was on behalf of Humphrey

Bogart he was not impressed. He was unhappy with yachtsmen

in general, and especially people from Beverly Hills. He told me

at length about his recent experience when he took his

grandchildren for a jeep ride to the only good sand beach on the

island, at Coches Prietos cove.

"A big power yacht was anchored off the beach and the

bastards were shooting at beer bottles they had lined up on the

sand," Stanton sputtered. "You know what I did? I got out my

binoculars and read her name and hailing port. It only took a

couple of days to find the owner's address in Beverly Hills, and a

couple more to arrange for a truck load of garbage to be dumped

on his front lawn," he said with pride. "He won't be leaving

Humphrey Bogart relaxing at anchor on SANTANA

broken glass on my grandkids' beach again!"

I assured Mr. Stanton that Mr. Bogart was a responsible, dependable, law-abiding citizen who would applaud the dump truck and do his best to educate other sailors about the rules of proper conduct at that beautiful island. Finally Stanton calmed down and agreed to issue a permit. One came through annually after that, with no fuss, and some of SANTANA's best times were spent at Santa Cruz.

Sailing regularly on SANTANA meant meeting interesting people; Bogie was involved with lots of unusual personalities from many fields. Most of them were from the arts but it didn't surprise me when some turned out to be from other sides of his life.

We had only visited the Los Angeles Yacht Club's anchorage in Howland's cove at Catalina a few times in several years after Bogie was accepted into the club. The moorings were reserved for more senior members, so we usually stayed in the less socially rigorous Moonstone cove farther down the island.

One Saturday afternoon we picked up an empty mooring in Howland's, planning to return his son Stephen and Jascha Heifetz's son to the mainland when they were released late Sunday morning from the boys camp there. It had been their first such experience, and Bogie was looking forward to sharing the sail back across the channel with his son, and I was excited about seeing the great violinist again. Before WWII he had played his special seagoing violin - made of aluminum - at a LAYC stag cruise, to a bunch of carousing sailors who gradually became quiet when they realized what was happening at their campfire. There was a hush when he played his last piece, the exquisite finale to many of his concerts... "The Londonderry Air" - known to most of us as "Danny Boy"...

Fifty yards away lay Bill Stewart's CHUBASCO, the de facto flagship of LAYC and the virtual descendant of SANTANA, but there was no recognition of our presence for half an hour or more, when someone on CHUBASCO stood up, waving, and shouted, "Bogie - is that you?"

Our captain, his first Scotch firmly in hand, stood up, squinted, and shouted back, "Pinky? It can't be!" It was.

"Pinky" DuPont and Humphrey Bogart had been classmates at Phillips Academy in Andover, Massachusetts, before America entered the first World War. Bogie had only stayed there briefly but apparently he was remembered, either for bad behavior or for flunking out - at different times he told several versions of his departure.

They exchanged cheerful greetings and insults, and Pinky came over later. He turned out to be a pleasant guest and a knowledgeable yachtsman who endeared himself to us with the comment that, "I could improve any ketch with a chain saw, but I love most yawls especially SANTANA and CHUBASCO!"

Sunday morning began in the usual way at the island. Quiet, peaceful, the very picture of yachting at its most enjoyable. We were sitting in the cockpit eating Roger's

60

magnificent breakfast of scrambled eggs and lobster when we realized the Commodore, on his majestic morning swim, was approaching SANTANA.

"Good morning, Bogie!" he said cordially, treading water a few feet away. Of course he was invited aboard, and he spent a few minutes telling us how happy he was that his old ship was there, what a nice day it was, and how pleased he was that his old friend Pinky and Bogie had been classmates.

As the Commodore swam away our captain wore a little smile. He had been a perfect host, sensing Stewart was changing his mind about the actor who had managed to join his club.

"I think it'll be different for us around here - Andover and the DuPonts matter to some of them," he muttered.

As Heifetz and Bogart had arranged, the great violinist arrived by plane and water taxi in time for us to pick the boys up in the dinghy at the camp's floating dock. They were glad to leave, eager to get home. Neither had been away at camp before, and this had been a rude experience for them. We dropped the mooring lines, made sail and headed toward San

Pedro as the Stewarts and Pinky waved cheerful goodbyes.

As SANTANA came out of the shelter of the island into

the dark blue seas of the open channel the big genoa jib began to

flap as it filled with wind, and the line controlling it snatched at

the winch. I put the handle on - and suddenly realized Jascha

Heifetz's fingers were an inch away from being crushed by the

heavy rope. He had done what any ordinary sailor would do,

taking slack out of the line, but it scared me.

"Watch out!" I barked. He barked back, glaring at me, "I

know how to use a winch!" and we brought the sail under

control.

Heifetz was right, of course. He was an experienced

sailor on his own gorgeous sloop SERENADE and it wasn't my

decision for him to pick up that rope. I wasn't responsible for his

fingers, he was, but I was very aware it was his left hand that

was in danger. I still wonder how I would feel if that line had

Celebrating the SANTANA's San Clemente Island Race win, Robert Dorris, Humphrey Bogart, Carl Petersen, Dean Harrell, Larry Dudley and John Freiburg.

caught one of his fingers and ended his incredible career ....

Stephen seemed ill at ease on the boat, at least the few times I saw him there. His father wanted him to become a sailor and looked forward to the time when Stephen could start lessons in a sailing dinghy, but he was too young to be comfortable on board and wanted to stay securely below most of the time. Bogie really didn't know how to relate to his son. He loved him, and his sister, but fatherhood had come late in Bogie's life and Stephen and Leslie didn't fit into it very well.

He was very aware of the problem, and tried to be the father he thought he should be. One Friday he came to SANTANA still chuckling about the confrontation he had with Stephen the night before. His son had behaved very badly at the dinner table, teasing Leslie unmercifully until she was sobbing. Bogie finally dragged him into the den and started on a loud, forceful bawling-out, complete with bulging veins and flying spittle.

Young Stephen Bogart on SANTANA.

"I was mad, and Stephen knew it. He listened seriously, looked up wide eyed, and said "You look just like a gorilla...."

"And of course, I did!" Bogie laughed.

He *could* laugh at himself, and seemed to be without many of the self-protective, ego boosting devices we tend to use to enhance our self-images.

When his long-time friend Erskine Johnson asked for help with his newspaper column Bogie supplied this:

THE KEYS TO THE KEELSON

By Humphrey Bogart

There are certain embarrassments that a movie actor has to face if he owns a boat. One of them is the business of having professional yachtsmen and boat owners look down their noses at upstart actors who clutter up the harbor and labor under the illusion that they are real sea-going characters.

Well seasoned sailors naturally cock a scornful eye at the Hollywood interlopers who arrive on the scene in clean, expensive dungarees and the inevitable captain's cap and proceed to prove how little they know about boating.

They usually have fine boats and the best equipment, and - fortunately - expert professional help in the operation of same.

But I can well see how it rankles veteran non-Hollywood yachtsmen to witness the spectacle of these playboy sailors making big talk about something most of them are pretty ignorant about.

I've tried to exercise restraint and pretend to be nothing more than an actor who sails and not a sailor who acts. This way I don't tread on the toes of my professional boating friends, who after all would be darned unwelcome if they came out to Warner Bros. and tried to tell me how to play a scene in "Chain Lightning. "

One of the greatest pleasures of sailing, as it is in golf or any other sport, comes in the clubhouse when the salt-water characters gather around to swap stories on the day's cruise or race or whatever. That's when an amateur has to watch his gab, or he'll give himself away as a marine moron, or he'll make himself unpopular with the professional if he starts shooting off his face.

I've been sailing off and on since I was a kid, so I'm not

68

exactly a newcomer on the water, but I've never been a

professional sailor (unless you call Navy service a profession),

and I've always tried to stay in my own class as a guy who

happens to sail for hobby purposes only. Sometimes, however,

I've probably unintentionally talked my way across the line into

the realm of the first team, but not for long because there's

always a silent, resentful reaction when you start talking big

among the big wheels of any business.

I'm not accusing every sea-going actor of being guilty of

trying to splash it up in boat circles, because a great many of

them appreciate the merits of non-invasion tactics and respect

the talent and ability of veteran boat-owners enough to stay out

of their hair. There are a few Hollywood people, however, who

think they know all the answers and consider themselves

qualified big shots in the nautical department. They don't know

any more about unfurling or making fast or skipping forward

than Lassie. And it's guys like these who give the entire movie

colony a D-rating along the docks.

Naturally every man takes pride in his boat and what she can do. I think, for example, that the SANTANA, a 55 foot yawl, is one of the best boats in the harbor for her size and type. And any man who doesn't brag about his boat is not a very good sailor. But I'm not just about to start telling my friends in San Pedro, Balboa and Newport how to operate their craft or what's wrong with them.

One thing special in boat circles is the puttering around that goes with boats. Whenever a boat is tied up in the slip the owner and crew spend many hours puttering with the paint brushes and the lines and canvas, and polishing brass. This is usually a silent, thoughtful process, and a sure way to distinguish an intruder from a veteran is by the amount of dialogue that goes on. Any conversation you have with the crew tied up alongside is generally businesslike and cut to a minimum. There's no idle gab when a sailor is puttering.

I have one inferiority complex about sailing. Only one. I'm not a good navigator. I know the SANTANA from stem to

70

stern and from port to starboard; I even know something about

engines and a lot about sails, and I'm pretty good at tacking. But

I can't navigate. If I don't have an expert navigator along, I

could very well start out for Ensenada and tie up at Santa

Barbara. This is an awful admission from a guy who sails as

much as some people sleep, but it's true.

My wife takes a bright attitude toward my navigating.

She says, "Never mind, Bogie. It's more fun that way, not

knowing where you are."

Bogart's sense of humor worked, even when he and

Betty wanted to start a family and they learned that his sperm

count was low. He needed a course of injections to build it up.

Accepting the situation as a medical necessity, he went in

regularly for the shots, remarking to the crew that he had bought

new, very colorful underwear so the nice nurse would not be

bored when he exposed his buttocks to her week after week.

Many months later she was a guest on a yacht anchored near us in White's cove at Catalina, and came aboard for a drink. We were all pleased to meet her and see the easy friendship they had established. Bogie could do that with almost anyone when he wanted to.

A couple of years after I started sailing with him Bogie demonstrated this charm for me. I was developing a good customer in the aircraft tooling business, who made drophammer dies used to form panels for Douglas Aircraft. He bought a lot of the special zinc alloy since the dies weighed up to several tons each.

Harold and his lady, Ann, were pleased when I chartered a nice, unremarkable little ketch to take them on their first sailing trip to Catalina. We anchored Saturday afternoon in the open part of the big bay called White's Landing, planning on a quiet weekend. An hour later I was surprised to see SANTANA come in to pick up her mooring in Moonstone cove, a few hundred

72

yards from us. As she passed us Bogie shouted an invitation to me to come aboard later for cocktails, and when I rowed over he asked if my friends would like to come along.

They spent the next two hours being charmed by one of the world's leading charmers, who made them feel completely at ease. There were drinks and hors d'oeuvres and pleasant talk without any mention of a business connection, but I sensed he understood the situation clearly. As we were getting into the dinghy Bogie said softly in my ear, "Did it help any, kid?" I assured him it would.

Harold never bought another pound of metal from our competitor and my boss was glad to approve the charter fee as justifiable entertainment expense, although he would prefer not to know about it in the future. "YACHT CHARTER doesn't seem as acceptable as MEALS AND DRINKS at good restaurants," he hinted.

Cruising weekends like that one were the way Bogie most often used his boat, without a plan or agenda.

Humphrey Bogart and Carl Petersen in a comedy routine.

We dinghied to friends' boats, or they came over to us to have a drink or a talk, or both. Someone aboard SANTANA seemed to know someone aboard a lot of the yachts nearby, and we had developed an easy exchange with many.

When Paul Mantz, then the leading stunt pilot for films, began to anchor his 80 foot motorsailer PEZ ESPADA near us they renewed a friendship that began on the set of *Jet Pilot* (which Bogie considered one of his worst pictures).

Paul loved to tell about the dummy fighter plane he had worked up for it, very clean lined and aerodynamically efficient-looking, but only intended to taxi around the field in close and medium shots.

"I could taxi pretty fast, then turn and stop with the brakes - gently - but it had no ailerons or rudder so it was a real shock when I came down the runway too fast and found the damn thing starting to take off. It was so clean it just wanted to fly!" he said proudly. He eased off on the throttle, touched back down without crashing, and made a friend of Bogie, who felt deep admiration for Mantz's skill - but gave him a hard time about the luxurious accommodations aboard PEZ ESPADA.

It was fun for three or four of us to go aboard on Sunday mornings and use Paul's electric toilets. Bogie explained that our simple, manually pumped ones made us feel so inferior we had to compensate by having several Bloody Marys mixed by Paul himself.

Another time we came into the cove during the week, when it was almost deserted, and found Paul and a couple of friends firing .22 pistols at cans thrown off the big yacht. After we picked up our mooring Bogie went over in the dinghy, planning to tell them to stop, but at the top of the boarding steps someone handed him a pistol and said, "Let's see if you really can shoot!"

Bogart whirled and fired from the hip, hitting the can, handed back the gun and went below without saying a word. He was having a hard time keeping a straight face, since he really didn't like guns and knew it was pure luck that he hit the can without aiming at all. He had only fired because of the challenge, but he never told Paul or his guest, who turned out to be a top writer from the SATURDAY EVENING POST doing a profile on Mantz.

Stories circulated in the magazine world for a long time about Humphrey Bogart's deadly shooting aim.

In settled summer weather SANTANA's usual mooring at Catalina was calm and quiet, off a pebbly beach where we would occasionally land from the dinghy to stretch our legs. Moonstone cove was leased to the Newport Harbor Yacht Club but other yachtsmen were free to use the moorings if club members didn't. An ever-changing roster of good boats came and went. and we were part of a relaxed, comfortable scene. Bogie would not have considered giving up his choice spot in the second row for anything - even if LAYC had offered him Bill Stewart's location in Howland's, eight miles west!

Beat the Devil, the last Huston picture he was in, left a bad taste in Bogie's mouth. The script John and his supposed collaborator, "James Helvick," were paid to write was non-existent, although Santana Productions had paid a lot of money for it. Bogie later decided the money had been spent on Huston's latest hobby, Irish fox hunting.

The script John was actually planning to shoot, by Peter Viertel and Tony Veiller, was doctored before and during production by Truman Capote, who happened to be in Italy and available. Bogie found himself liking this unusual little man, and they became good friends. Bogie saw that Tru had brought at least some order to the confusion on the set, but a year later he was still very unhappy with the whole enterprise.

"I knocked out my front teeth and bit my tongue in a dumb car crash, had to smell Gina's garlic in the close ups, waited for rewrites while John stalled with camera setups - on my money - and I could never figure out what was supposed to be happening," he groused. "Betty and Tru and Peter Lorre kept me sane, but I think anybody who says he likes that kind of absurd, campy, pointless crap is a phony!"

78

It became a kind of litmus test - Bogie would ask someone what they thought of *Beat the Devil*, and if it was even hinted that it was a good picture they went on his PHONY list.

Since directors were so important to him, Bogie had strong feelings about some of them. He had worked for a lot of the best, a few of the worst and many of the mediocre on nearly 75 films in more than 25 years. He firmly believed the director should run the picture, and apparently he usually took direction well, trying to give the performance the man wanted. Even when he found it hard to understand William Wyler's style - repeated takes without telling the actors what was wrong, just "Do it again," - he trusted Wyler to know when they had it right, and usually worked without complaint. "Somebody has to be in charge," he said.

On the other hand, there were directors and actors he would rather not work with. One Friday evening he arrived at SANTANA obviously still upset over his day on the Sabrina set.

He was uncomfortable playing the stuffy Linus, didn't get along with Billy Wilder, and was not a great fan of Bill Holden's. The tension between the three of them was heightened by Audrey Hepburn's nervousness, which caused repeated takes.

Bogie had a well-earned reputation for knowing his lines, having developed a remarkable ability to read almost anything and give it back word for word. I knew how he had prepared for the FCC test for SANTANA's high seas radio license, scanning the technical manual at high speed. The next day he passed the test easily. He told me that in another day he would have forgotten most of it, but he could and did retain things that mattered, like the yacht racing rules!

Hepburn had blown her lines in one scene repeatedly. After 10 or 12 takes he had finally muttered something like, "And she calls herself an actress!" Wilder and Holden leaped to her defense, Hepburn burst into tears, and the day ended very badly.

Bogie could be very tough on people he felt were

unprofessional - not prepared by natural, instinctive ability or by training to meet the needs of a movie, play or radio show. He didn't mind rehearsals, or repeated takes if the point was to do it better, but he had little patience when scenes were spoiled by someone simply losing their lines.

Warren Stevens, a young Method actor from New York, had been cast in his first, film, *The Barefoot Contessa*. He was nervous about working with Bogart and director Joseph Mankiewicz, who could be hard on actors, and a few years later told Carol and me about his first day on the set.

"Bogie and I did the scene a couple of times, the director said, 'Print it,' and they started to break down the setup. I felt sure I could have done it better, so I asked for another take, which was very graciously granted.

"After that one I was sure it could be even better; at least I could be better, so I asked for another, and another. Then Bogie quietly called me aside and said, 'You know, kid, if it makes you feel good we could do this scene all afternoon, but you should know there hasn't been any film in the camera since Joe said "Print it." He's in charge – and we're being very nice to you.'

"It was my first and best lesson in film making. Bogie had done the scene well every time, working with me through my variations and uncertainties, knowing I was trying hard to improve, but at the end he wanted me to know whose judgment really mattered."

Bogie didn't mind doing exercises with a serious actor, but he hated 12 takes with an actress who couldn't remember a few lines. Perhaps he should have been more forgiving, but he and his old friends from the theater had rather rigid standards for pros. "If you take the money you'd better learn your lines and hit your marks," was his feeling.

THE LAST YEARS

At the Midwinter Regatta in early February 1956 Bogie's usual cough was worse. He seemed distracted, less interested in the racing than he had always been, and he finally told me he was going in for an exploratory look at his esophagus, where he had been feeling some pain. He obviously didn't want to talk much about it.

Two months later he was supposed to be recovering from the surgery, which had left him weak and tired, but when we met on SANTANA it was plain that the strain of therapy was telling on him. Although he talked about getting her out of the slip, it was clear he was not going to be using the boat much in the near future - but we kept making vague plans for the coming summer's cruising.

"Maybe we can get back to Santa Cruz," he mused. "I'd like Stephen to see it..."

As his visits to San Pedro became less frequent he began

to need a male nurse/chauffeur to drive there, and he depended more and more on reports on her condition.

When I called he wanted news about the ship and the crew, and his first question was usually, "Is Carl doing his duty or is he fucking off?" He wanted me to remind Carl of the Viking funeral they had joked about so many times ... yet he never really gave anyone an opening to even imply that he was not going to get well. He earned respect, not sympathy.

It appeared that unless he improved he would not be able to go out on SANTANA, but he surprised us in midsummer with an invitation to spend a weekend at Newport Harbor Yacht Club, where he had sent Carl with the boat. He never talked about why he wanted to be there, but it must have been for a brief reminder of the time in '44 and '45 when he and Betty and SANTANA came together, and the happiest years of his life began.

Carol and I were prepared for a weakened but still functioning captain, but not for his drastic loss of weight. It was frightening to see him so gaunt, but when we made a brief visit

Humphrey Bogart at the helm of SANTANA.

to the club bar he spoke to several friends as if he was in the best of shape. No one said a word about his appearance. It was as if Bogie was challenging them to make a remark, and no one did.

That evening Carl called me aside to explain the great effort Bogie had made for this weekend. He was freshly shaven, dressed in his best, cleanest boat clothes - and he made a special point of trying to eat the tamale pie he had asked Carol to bring, another reminder of good times. He couldn't swallow more than a bite, but he tried.

On Sunday SANTANA went out of the harbor for a short sail. Bob Marlatt and Cal Smith's wife - "The Mormon" Bogie always called her - were along as we found a light breeze and reached slowly offshore a few miles. Bogie sat by himself in the cockpit looking at the sea, not saying anything as Carl and Bob and I sailed as smoothly and well as we could. No one talked much. We all knew it was Bogie's last sail on his beloved boat.

SANTANA went back to San Pedro and Carol and I waited for calls from Betty. Bogie wanted to see his friends, and we were glad to come in, sometimes on short notice, from Topanga Canyon.

Betty set increasingly tight limits on visits. At first we went upstairs to their bedroom and sat close to him, but soon she established the "Evenings in the Den" routine that became the focal point of his day. By the time we arrived Bogie would be settled into his chair, token Martini in hand, Harvey, the ever-present boxer nearby, and the brief - not over 15 or 20 minutes - visit started.

We talked about the boat a bit, but more about families and friends and children. Carol and I were still excited about the birth of our fourth child, Jim, in late September, and I received a lot of un-asked-for advice about vasectomies from Betty, who quoted Bill Holden as saying his had made a positive change in his life.

As the months went by Bogie began to stay in the

wheelchair he had ridden down the dumbwaiter from the upstairs hall. His drinks got even weaker. He never complained, tried to put us at ease, and suffered constantly.

A couple of weeks after Christmas Betty called, a special note in her voice, asking us to come in Saturday evening. We found him weaker than ever, sometimes drifting into brief periods of semi- coma, but he was still the considerate man we loved. Since we now lived in Topanga, which he considered a wilderness far to the west (actually only a half hour drive away) he was concerned that as bumpkins we might not go to a good restaurant when we left.

He kept telling Betty to call Dino's so we could get some good Italian food, and we kept trying to reassure him that we would be fine.

Just before we left him he said weakly to me, "Too bad, I never got you together with Kate, did I…it would have been fun to hear you two…"

As we left Betty came to the front door and gave us each

a hard hug. "It won't be much longer," she sobbed, very softly.

Her incredible courage and love had carried her to the end.

Minutes after we drove away Spencer and Kate arrived for their last visit.

Humphrey DeForest Bogart died peacefully early Monday morning, January 14, 1957.

All Saints Episcopal Church with the model of SANTANA

THE MEMORIAL SERVICE

The memorial service itself was held at 11:30am on Thursday the 17th at All Saint's Episcopal Church, in Beverly Hills. Bogie requested to be cremated and have his ashes scattered in the Pacific from the deck of SANTANA, but that was not allowed at the time. So Betty did the next best thing and had Bogie's scale model of his beloved yawl SANTANA placed front and center at the service.

I could not have been given a greater honor than to serve as one of Bogie's pallbearers.

Over three thousand spectators showed up, and guests included Katharine Hepburn, Spencer Tracy, David Niven, Ronald Reagan, James Mason, Danny Kaye, Joan Fontaine, Marlene Dietrich, Errol Flynn, Gregory Peck, and Gary Cooper, as well as Billy Wilder and Jack Warner, and of course, the family. John Huston eulogized his friend with the words,

"Himself, he never took too seriously—his work most seriously. He regarded the somewhat gaudy figure of Bogart, the star, with an amused cynicism; Bogart, the actor, he held in deep respect...In each of the fountains at Versailles there is a pike which keeps all the carp active; otherwise they would grow overfat and die. Bogie took rare delight in performing a similar duty in the fountains of Hollywood...He is quite irreplaceable. There will never be another like him."

CPSIA information can be obtained
at www.ICGtesting.com
Printed in the USA
LVOW10s1959270717

542871LV00020B/319/P